CONVENTION BETWEEN
THE GOVERNMENT OF THE UNITED STATES OF AMERICA
AND
THE GOVERNMENT OF THE ITALIAN REPUBLIC
FOR THE AVOIDANCE OF DOUBLE TAXATION
WITH RESPECT TO TAXES ON INCOME
AND THE PREVENTION OF FRAUD OR FISCAL EVASION

CONVENTION BETWEEN
THE GOVERNMENT OF THE UNITED STATES OF AMERICA
AND
THE GOVERNMENT OF THE ITALIAN REPUBLIC
FOR THE AVOIDANCE OF DOUBLE TAXATION
WITH RESPECT TO TAXES ON INCOME
AND THE PREVENTION OF FRAUD OR FISCAL EVASION

The Government of the United States of America and the Government of the Italian Republic, desiring to conclude a Convention for the avoidance of double taxation with respect to taxes on income and the prevention of fraud or fiscal evasion, have agreed as follows:

ARTICLE 1

Personal Scope

1. Except as otherwise provided in this Convention, this Convention shall apply to persons who are residents of one or both of the Contracting States.

2. Notwithstanding any provision of this Convention except paragraph 3 of this Article, a Contracting State may tax:

(a) its residents (as determined under Article 4 (Resident); and

(b) its citizens by reason of citizenship as if there were no convention between the Government of the United States of America and the Government of the Italian Republic for the avoidance of double taxation with respect to taxes on income and the prevention of fraud or fiscal evasion.

3. The provisions of paragraph 2 shall not affect:

(a) the benefits conferred by a Contracting State under paragraph 2 of Article 9 (Associated Enterprises), paragraphs 5 and 6 of Article 18 (Pensions, Etc.), and under Articles 23 (Relief from Double Taxation), 24 (Non-Discrimination), and 25 (Mutual Agreement Procedure); and

(b) the benefits conferred by a Contracting State under Articles 19 (Government Service), 20 (Professors and Teachers), 21 (Students and Trainees), and 27 (Diplomatic Agents and Consular Officials), upon individuals who are neither citizens of, nor have immigrant status in, that State.

ARTICLE 2

Taxes Covered

1. This Convention shall apply to taxes on income imposed on behalf of a Contracting State.

2. The existing taxes to which this Convention shall apply are:

(a) in the case of the United States: the Federal income taxes imposed by the Internal Revenue Code (but excluding social security taxes), and the Federal excise taxes imposed on insurance premiums paid to foreign insurers and with respect to private foundations (hereinafter referred to as "United States tax");

(b) in the case of Italy:

(i) the individual income tax (l'imposta sul reddito delle persone fisiche);

(ii) the corporation income tax (l'imposta sul reddito delle persone giuridiche); and

(iii) the regional tax on productive activities (l'imposta regionale sulle attività produttive), but only that portion of such tax that is considered to be an income tax pursuant to paragraph 2(c) of Article 23 (Relief from Double Taxation);

even if they are collected by withholding taxes at the source (hereinafter referred to as "Italian tax").

3. The Convention shall apply also to any identical or substantially similar taxes which are imposed by a Contracting State after the date of signature of this Convention in addition

to, or in place of, the existing taxes. The competent authorities of the Contracting States shall notify each other of any significant changes which have been made in their respective taxation laws and shall transmit to each other any significant official published material concerning the application of this Convention, including explanations, regulations, rulings, or judicial decisions.

ARTICLE 3

General Definitions

1. For the purposes of this Convention, unless the context otherwise requires:

(a) the term "person" includes an individual, a company, an estate, a trust, a partnership, and any other body of persons;

(b) the term "company" means any body corporate or any entity which is treated as a body corporate for tax purposes;

(c) the terms "enterprise of a Contracting State" and "enterprise of the other Contracting State" mean respectively an enterprise carried on by a resident of a Contracting State and an enterprise carried on by a resident of the other Contracting State;

(d) the term "international traffic" means any transport by a ship or aircraft, except where such transport is solely between places in the other Contracting State;

(e) the term "competent authority" means:

(i) in the United States: the Secretary of the Treasury or his delegate; and

(ii) in Italy: the Ministry of Finance;

(f) the term "United States" means the United States of America, and includes the states thereof and the District of Columbia; such term also includes the territorial sea thereof and any area beyond the territorial sea which is designated as an area within which the United States, in compliance with its legislation and in conformity with international law, exercises sovereign rights in respect of the exploration and exploitation of the natural resources of the seabed, the subsoil and the superjacent waters; the term, however, does not include Puerto Rico, the Virgin Islands, Guam or any other United States possession or territory;

(g) the term "Italy" means the Italian Republic and includes any area beyond the territorial sea which is designated as an area within which Italy, in compliance with its legislation and in conformity with international law, exercises sovereign rights in respect of the exploration and exploitation of the natural resources of the seabed, the subsoil and the superjacent waters;

(h) the term "nationals" means:

(i) all individuals possessing the citizenship of a Contracting State; and

(ii) all legal persons, partnerships, and associations deriving their status as such from the law in force in a Contracting State.

(i) the term "qualified governmental entity" means:

(i) any person or body of persons that constitutes a governing body of a Contracting State, or of a political or administrative subdivision or local authority of a Contracting State;

(ii) a person that is wholly owned, directly or indirectly, by a Contracting State or a political or administrative subdivision or local authority of a Contracting State, provided (A) it is organized under the laws of the Contracting State, (B) its earnings are credited to its own account with no portion of its income inuring to the benefit of any private person, and (C) its assets vest in the Contracting State, political or administrative subdivision or local authority upon dissolution; and

(iii) a pension trust or fund of a person described in subparagraph (i) or (ii) that is
constituted and operated exclusively to administer or
provide pension benefits described in Article 19
(Government Service);

provided that an entity described in subparagraph (ii) or
(iii) does not carry on commercial activities.

2. As regards the application of this Convention by a
Contracting State any term not defined therein shall, unless the
context otherwise requires, have the meaning which it has under
the laws of that State concerning the taxes to which this
Convention applies.

ARTICLE 4

Resident

1. For purposes of this Convention, the term "resident of a
Contracting State" means any person who, under the laws of that
State, is liable to tax therein by reason of his domicile,
residence, place of management, place of incorporation, or any
other criterion of a similar nature, provided, however, that:

(a) this term does not include any person who is
liable to tax in that State in respect only of income from
sources in that State; and

(b) in the case of income derived or paid by a
partnership, estate, or trust, this term applies only to
the extent that the income derived by such partnership,
estate, or trust is subject to tax in that State, either in
its hands or in the hands of its partners or beneficiaries.

2. Where by reason of the provisions of paragraph 1 an
individual is a resident of both Contracting States, then his
status shall be determined as follows:

(a) he shall be deemed to be a resident of the State
in which he has a permanent home available to him; if he
has a permanent home available to him in both States, he
shall be deemed to be a resident of that State with which

his personal and economic relations are closer (center of vital interests);

    (b) if the State in which he has his center of vital interests cannot be determined, or if he has not a permanent home available to him in either State, he shall be deemed to be a resident of the State in which he has an habitual abode;

    (c) if he has an habitual abode in both States or in neither of them, he shall be deemed to be a resident of the State of which he is a national;

    (d) if he is a national of both States or neither of them, the competent authorities of the Contracting States shall settle the question by mutual agreement.

3. Where by reason of the provisions of paragraph 1 a person other than an individual is a resident of both Contracting States, the competent authorities of the Contracting States shall by mutual agreement endeavor to settle the question and to determine the mode of application of the Convention to such person.

ARTICLE 5

Permanent Establishment

1. For the purposes of this Convention, the term "permanent establishment" means a fixed place of business in which the business of the enterprise is wholly or partly carried on.

2. The term "permanent establishment" shall include especially:

    (a) a place of management;
    (b) a branch;
    (c) an office;
    (d) a factory;
    (e) a workshop;
    (f) a mine, quarry, or other place of extraction of natural resources; and
    (g) a building site or construction or assembly project which exists for more than twelve months;

3. The term "permanent establishment" shall be deemed not to include:

    (a) the use of facilities solely for the purpose of storage, display, or delivery of goods or merchandise belonging to the enterprise;

    (b) the maintenance of a stock of goods or merchandise belonging to the enterprise solely for the purpose of storage, display, or delivery;

    (c) the maintenance of a stock of goods or merchandise belonging to the enterprise solely for the purpose of processing by another enterprise;

    (d) the maintenance of a fixed place of business solely for the purpose of purchasing goods or merchandise, or for collecting information, for the enterprise;

    (e) the maintenance of a fixed place of business solely for the purpose of advertising, for the supply of information, for scientific research, or for similar activities which have a preparatory or auxiliary character, for the enterprise.

4. A person acting in a Contracting State on behalf of an enterprise of the other Contracting State -- other than an agent of an independent status to whom paragraph 5 applies -- shall be deemed to be a permanent establishment in the first-mentioned State if he has, and habitually exercises in that State, an authority to conclude contracts in the name of the enterprise, unless his activities are limited to the purchase of goods or merchandise for the enterprise.

5. An enterprise of a Contracting State shall not be deemed to have a permanent establishment in the other Contracting State merely because it carries on business in that other State through a broker, general commission agent, or any other agent of an independent status, where such persons are acting in the ordinary course of their business as independent agents.

6. The fact that a company which is a resident of a Contracting State controls or is controlled by a company which is a resident of the other Contracting State, or which carries on business in that other State (whether through a permanent

establishment or otherwise), shall not of itself constitute either company a permanent establishment of the other.

ARTICLE 6

Income from Immovable Property

1. Income derived by a resident of a Contracting State from immovable property, including income from agriculture or forestry, situated in the other Contracting State may be taxed in that other State.

2. The term "immovable property" ("real property") shall have the meaning which it has under the law of the Contracting State in which the property in question is situated. The term shall in any case include property accessory to immovable property, livestock and equipment used in agriculture and forestry, and rights to which the provisions of general law respecting landed property apply. Usufruct of immovable property and rights to variable or fixed payments as consideration for the working of, or the right to work, mineral deposits, sources, and other natural resources shall also be considered immovable property; ships, boats, and aircraft shall not be regarded as immovable property.

3. The provisions of paragraph 1 shall apply to income derived from the direct use, letting, or use in any other form of immovable property.

4. The provisions of paragraphs 1 and 3 shall also apply to the income from immovable property of an enterprise and to income from immovable property used for the performance of independent personal services.

ARTICLE 7

Business Profits

1. The profits of an enterprise of a Contracting State shall be taxable only in that State unless the enterprise carries on business in the other Contracting State through a permanent establishment situated therein. If the enterprise carries on business as aforesaid, the profits of the enterprise

may be taxed in the other State but only so much of them as is attributable to that permanent establishment.

2. Subject to the provisions of paragraph 3, where an enterprise of a Contracting State carries on business in the other Contracting State through a permanent establishment situated therein, there shall in each Contracting State be attributed to that permanent establishment the profits which it might be expected to make if it were a distinct and separate enterprise engaged in the same or similar activities under the same or similar conditions and dealing wholly independently with the enterprise of which it is a permanent establishment and other associated enterprises.

3. In determining the profits of a permanent establishment, there shall be allowed as deductions expenses that are attributable to the activities of the permanent establishment, including a reasonable allocation of executive and general administrative expenses, whether incurred in the State in which the permanent establishment is situated or elsewhere.

4. No profits shall be attributable to a permanent establishment by reason of the mere purchase by that permanent establishment of goods or merchandise for the enterprise.

5. For the purposes of the preceding paragraphs, the profits to be attributed to the permanent establishment shall be determined by the same method year by year unless there is good and sufficient reason to the contrary.

6. In applying paragraphs 1 and 2 of Article 7 (Business Profits), paragraph 4 of Article 10 (Dividends), paragraph 5 of Article 11 (Interest), paragraph 5 of Article 12 (Royalties), paragraph 2 of Article 13 (Capital Gains), Article 14 (Independent Personal Services) and paragraph 2 of Article 22 (Other Income), any income or gain attributable to a permanent establishment or fixed base during its existence is taxable in the Contracting State where such permanent establishment or fixed base is situated even if the payments are deferred until after such permanent establishment or fixed base has ceased to exist.

7. Where profits include items of income which are dealt with separately in other Articles of this Convention, then the provisions of those Articles shall not be affected by the provisions of this Article.

ARTICLE 8

Shipping and Air Transport

1. Profits of an enterprise of a Contracting State from the operation in international traffic of ships or aircraft shall be taxable only in that State.

2. The provisions of paragraph 1 shall also apply to profits derived from the participation in a pool, a joint business, or an international operating agency.

ARTICLE 9

Associated Enterprises

1. Where:

   (a) an enterprise of a Contracting State participates directly or indirectly in the management, control, or capital of an enterprise of the other Contracting State; or

   (b) the same persons participate directly or indirectly in the management, control, or capital of an enterprise of a Contracting State and an enterprise of the other Contracting State,

and in either case conditions are made or imposed between the two enterprises in their commercial or financial relations which differ from those which would be made between independent enterprises, then any profits which would, but for those conditions, have accrued to one of the enterprises, but, by reason of those conditions, have not so accrued, may be included in the profits of that enterprise and taxed accordingly.

2. Where a Contracting State includes in the profits of an enterprise of that State - and taxes accordingly - profits on which an enterprise of the other Contracting State has been charged to tax in that other State and the profits so included are profits which would have accrued to the enterprise of the first-mentioned State if the conditions made between the two enterprises had been those which would have been made between

independent enterprises, then that other State shall make an appropriate adjustment to the amount of the tax charged therein on those profits. In determining such adjustment, due regard shall be had to the other provisions of this Convention and, in any case, any such adjustment shall be made only in accordance with the mutual agreement procedure in Article 25 (Mutual Agreement Procedure) of the Convention.

ARTICLE 10

Dividends

1. Dividends paid by a company which is a resident of a Contracting State to a resident of the other Contracting State may be taxed in that other State.

2. However, such dividends may also be taxed in the Contracting State of which the company paying the dividends is a resident and according to the laws of that State, but if the beneficial owner of the dividends is a resident of the other Contracting State, the tax so charged shall not exceed:

   (a) 5 percent of the gross amount of the dividends if the beneficial owner is a company which has owned at least 25 percent of the voting stock of the company paying the dividends for a 12 month period ending on the date the dividend is declared; and

   (b) 15 percent of the gross amount of the dividends in all other cases.

This paragraph shall not affect the taxation of the company in respect of the profits out of which the dividends are paid.

3. The term "dividends" as used in this Article means income from shares, "jouissance" shares or "jouissance" rights, mining shares, founder's shares, or other rights, not being debt-claims, participating in profits, as well as income which is subjected to the same taxation treatment as income from shares by the laws of the State of which the company making the distribution is a resident.

4. The provisions of paragraphs 1 and 2 shall not apply if the beneficial owner of the dividends, being a resident of a

Contracting State, carries on business in the other Contracting State, of which the company paying the dividends is a resident, through a permanent establishment situated therein, or performs in that other State independent personal services from a fixed base situated therein, and the holding in respect of which the dividends are paid is effectively connected with such permanent establishment or fixed base. In such case, the dividends are taxable in that other Contracting State according to its own laws.

5. Where a company which is a resident of a Contracting State and not a resident of the other Contracting State derives profits or income from the other Contracting State, that other State may not impose any tax on the dividends paid by the company, except insofar as such dividends are paid to a resident of that other State or insofar as the holding in respect of which the dividends are paid is effectively connected with a permanent establishment or a fixed base situated in that other State, nor subject the company's undistributed profits to a tax on the company's undistributed profits, except as provided in paragraph 6, even if the dividends paid or the undistributed profits consist wholly or partly of profits or income arising in such other State.

6. A corporation that is a resident of one of the States and that has a permanent establishment in the other State or that is subject to tax in the other State on a net basis on its income that may be taxed in the other State under Article 6 (Income from Immovable Property) or under paragraph 1 of Article 13 (Capital Gains) may be subject in that other State to a tax in addition to the tax allowable under the other provisions of this Convention. Such tax, however, may be imposed on only the portion of the business profits of the corporation attributable to the permanent establishment and the portion of the income referred to in the preceding sentence that is subject to tax under Article 6 (Income from Immovable Property) or under paragraph 1 of Article 13 (Capital Gains) that, in the case of the United States, represents the dividend equivalent amount of such profits or income and, in the case of Italy, is an amount that is analogous to the dividend equivalent amount.

7. The tax referred to in paragraph 6 may not be imposed at a rate in excess of the rate specified in paragraph 2(a).

8. Notwithstanding paragraph 2, dividends shall not be taxed in the Contracting State of which the company paying the

dividends is a resident if the beneficial owner of the dividends is a resident of the other Contracting State that is a qualified governmental entity that holds, directly or indirectly, less than 25 percent of the voting stock of the company paying the dividends.

9. Subparagraph (a) of paragraph 2 shall not apply in the case of dividends paid by a United States Regulated Investment Company (RIC) or a United States Real Estate Investment Trust (REIT). In the case of dividends from a RIC, subparagraph (b) of paragraph 2 shall apply. In the case of dividends paid by a REIT, subparagraph (b) of paragraph 2 shall apply only if:

(a) the beneficial owner of the dividends is an individual holding an interest of not more than 10 percent in the REIT;

(b) the dividends are paid with respect to a class of stock that is publicly traded and the beneficial owner of the dividends is a person holding an interest of not more than 5 percent of any class of the REIT's stock; or

(c) the beneficial owner of the dividends is a person holding an interest of not more than 10 percent in the REIT and the REIT is diversified.

10. The provisions of this Article shall not apply if it was the main purpose or one of the main purposes of any person concerned with the creation or assignment of the shares or other rights in respect of which the dividend is paid to take advantage of this Article by means of that creation or assignment.

ARTICLE 11

Interest

1. Interest arising in a Contracting State and paid to a resident of the other Contracting State may be taxed in that other State.

2. However, such interest may also be taxed in the Contracting State in which it arises and according to the laws of that State, but if the beneficial owner of the interest is a

resident of the other Contracting State, the tax so charged shall not exceed 10 percent of the gross amount of the interest.

3.   Notwithstanding paragraph 2, interest shall not be taxed in the Contracting State in which it arises if:

(a) the interest is beneficially owned by a resident of the other Contracting State that is a qualified governmental entity that holds, directly or indirectly, less than 25 percent of the capital of the person paying the interest;

(b) the interest is paid with respect to debt obligations guaranteed or insured by a qualified governmental entity of that Contracting State or the other Contracting State and is beneficially owned by a resident of the other Contracting State;

(c) the interest is paid or accrued with respect to a sale on credit of goods, merchandise, or services provided by one enterprise to another enterprise; or

(d) the interest is paid or accrued in connection with the sale on credit of industrial, commercial, or scientific equipment.

4. The term "interest" as used in this Article means income from Government securities, bonds, or debentures, whether or not secured by mortgage and whether or not carrying a right to participate in profits, and debt-claims of every kind as well as all other income assimilated to income from money lent by the taxation law of the State in which the income arises. Income dealt with in Article 10 (Dividends) shall not be regarded as interest for the purposes of this Convention.

5. The provisions of paragraphs 1, 2, and 3 shall not apply if the beneficial owner of the interest, being a resident of a Contracting State, carries on business in the other Contracting State in which the interest arises, through a permanent establishment situated therein, or performs in that other State independent personal service from a fixed base situated therein, and the debt-claim in respect of which the interest is paid is effectively connected with such permanent establishment or fixed base. In such case, the interest is taxable in that other Contracting State according to its own laws.

6. Interest shall be deemed to arise in a Contracting State when the payer is that State itself, a political or administrative subdivision, a local authority, or a resident of that State. Where, however, the person paying the interest, whether he is a resident of a Contracting State or not, has in a Contracting State a permanent establishment or a fixed base in connection with which the indebtedness on which the interest is paid was incurred, and such interest is borne by such permanent establishment or fixed base, then such interest shall be deemed to arise in the State in which the permanent establishment or fixed base is situated.

7. Where, by reason of a special relationship between the payer and the beneficial owner or between both of them and some other person, the amount of the interest, having regard to the debt-claim for which it is paid, exceeds the amount which would have been agreed upon by the payer and the beneficial owner in the absence of such relationship, the provisions of this Article shall apply only to the last-mentioned amount. In such case, the excess part of the payments is taxable according to the laws of each Contracting State, due regard being had to the other provisions of this Convention.

8. In the case of the United States, the excess, if any, of the amount of interest allocable to the profits of a company resident in the other Contracting State that are either attributable to a permanent establishment in the United States or subject to tax in the United States under Article 6 (Income from Immovable Property) or paragraph 1 of Article 13 (Capital Gains) over the interest paid by that permanent establishment or trade or business in the United States shall be deemed to arise in the United States and be beneficially owned by a resident of the other Contracting State. The tax imposed under this Article on such interest shall not exceed the rate specified in paragraph 2.

9. The provisions of this Article shall not apply if it was the main purpose or one of the main purposes of any person concerned with the creation or assignment of the debt-claim in respect of which the interest is paid to take advantage of this Article by means of that creation or assignment.

ARTICLE 12

Royalties

1. Royalties arising in a Contracting State and paid to a resident of the other Contracting State may be taxed in that other State.

2. However, such royalties may also be taxed in the Contracting State in which they arise and according to the laws of that State, but if the recipient of the royalties is the beneficial owner thereof, the tax so charged shall not exceed:

(a) 5 percent of the gross amount in the case of royalties for the use of, or the right to use, computer software or industrial, commercial, or scientific equipment; and

(b) 8 percent of the gross amount in all other cases.

3. Notwithstanding the provisions of paragraph 2, royalties arising in a State and paid to a resident of the other State for the use of, or right to use, a copyright of literary, artistic or scientific work (excluding royalties for computer software, motion pictures, films, tapes or other means of reproduction used for radio or television broadcasting) shall be taxable only in that other State if such resident is the beneficial owner thereof.

4. The term "royalties" as used in this Article means payments of any kind received as a consideration for the use of, or the right to use, any copyright of literary, artistic, or scientific work including computer software, motion pictures, films, tapes or other means of reproduction used for radio or television broadcasting, any patent, trademark, design or model, plan, secret formula or process, or other like right or property, or for the use of, or right to use, industrial, commercial, or scientific equipment, or for information concerning industrial, commercial, or scientific experience.

5. The provisions of paragraphs 1, 2, and 3 shall not apply if the beneficial owner of the royalties, being a resident of a Contracting State, carries on business in the other Contracting State in which the royalties arise, through a permanent establishment situated therein, or performs in that other State independent personal services from a fixed base situated

therein, and the right or property in respect of which the royalties are paid is effectively connected with such permanent establishment or fixed base. In such case, the royalties are taxable in that other Contracting State according to its own laws.

6. Royalties shall be deemed to arise in a Contracting State when the payer is that State itself, a political or administrative subdivision, a local authority, or a resident of that State. Where, however, the person paying the royalties, whether he is a resident of a Contracting State or not, has in a Contracting State a permanent establishment or a fixed base in connection with which the obligation to pay the royalties was incurred, and such royalties are borne by such permanent establishment or fixed base, then such royalties shall be deemed to arise in the State in which the permanent establishment or fixed base is situated. Notwithstanding the preceding provisions of this paragraph, royalties with respect to the use of, or the right to use, rights or property within a Contracting State may be deemed to arise within that State.

7. Where, by reason of a special relationship between the payer and the beneficial owner or between both of them and some other person, the amount of the royalties, having regard to the use, right, or information for which they are paid, exceeds the amount which would have been agreed upon by the payer and the beneficial owner in the absence of such relationship, the provisions of this Article shall apply only to the last-mentioned amount. In such case, the excess part of the payments is taxable according to the laws of each Contracting State, due regard being had to the other provisions of this Convention.

8. The provisions of this Article shall not apply if it was the main purpose or one of the main purposes of any person concerned with the creation or assignment of the rights in respect of which the royalties are paid to take advantage of this Article by means of that creation or assignment.

ARTICLE 13

Capital Gains

1. Gains derived by a resident of a Contracting State from the alienation of immovable property situated in the other Contracting State may be taxed in that other State.

2. Gains from the alienation of movable property forming part of the business property of a permanent establishment which an enterprise of a Contracting State has in the other Contracting State or of movable property pertaining to a fixed base available to a resident of a Contracting State in the other Contracting State for the purpose of performing independent personal services, including such gains from the alienation of such permanent establishment (alone or with the whole enterprise) or of such fixed base, may be taxed in that other State.

3. Gains derived by an enterprise of a Contracting State from the alienation of ships or aircraft operated by such enterprise in international traffic or of movable property pertaining to the operation of such ships or aircraft shall be taxable only in that State.

4. Gains from the alienation of any property other than that referred to in paragraphs 1, 2, and 3 shall be taxable only in the Contracting State of which the alienator is a resident.

ARTICLE 14

Independent Personal Services

1. Income derived by an individual who is a resident of a Contracting State from the performance of personal services in an independent capacity shall be taxable only in that State unless such services are performed in the other Contracting State and the individual has a fixed base regularly available to him in that other State for the purpose of performing his activities, but only so much of the income as is attributable to that fixed base may be taxed in that other State.

2. The term "personal services in an independent capacity" includes, but is not limited to, scientific, literary, artistic,

educational, and teaching activities as well as independent activities of physicians, lawyers, engineers, architects, dentists, and accountants.

ARTICLE 15

Dependent Personal Services

1. Subject to the provisions of Articles 16 (Directors' Fees), 18 (Pensions, Etc.), 19 (Government Service), 20 (Professors and Teachers), and 21 (Students and Trainees), salaries, wages, and other similar remuneration derived by a resident of a Contracting State in respect of an employment shall be taxable only in that State unless the employment is exercised in the other Contracting State. If the employment is so exercised, such remuneration as is derived therefrom may be taxed in that other State.

2. Notwithstanding the provisions of paragraph 1, remuneration derived by a resident of a Contracting State in respect of an employment exercised in the other Contracting State shall be taxable only in the first-mentioned State if:

    (a) the recipient is present in the other State for a period or periods not exceeding in the aggregate 183 days in the fiscal year concerned;

    (b) the remuneration is paid by, or on behalf of, an employer who is not a resident of the other State; and

    (c) the remuneration is not borne by a permanent establishment or a fixed base which the employer has in the other State.

3. Notwithstanding the preceding provisions of this Article, remuneration in respect of an employment regularly exercised aboard a ship or aircraft operated in international traffic by an enterprise of a Contracting State may be taxed in that State.

ARTICLE 16

Directors' Fees

Directors' fees and other similar payments derived by a resident of a Contracting State in his capacity as a member of the board of directors of a company which is a resident of the other Contracting State may be taxed in that other State.

ARTICLE 17

Artistes and Athletes

1. Income derived by a resident of a Contracting State as an entertainer, such as a theatre, motion picture, radio, or television artiste, or a musician, or as an athlete, from his personal activities as such exercised in the other Contracting State, which income would be exempt from tax in that other Contracting State under the provisions of Articles 14 (Independent Personal Services) and 15 (Dependent Personal Services), may be taxed in that other State, if:

    (a) the amount of the gross receipts derived by such entertainer or athlete, including expenses reimbursed to him or borne on his behalf, from such activities exceeds twenty thousand United States dollars ($20,000) or its equivalent in Italian currency for the fiscal year concerned; or

    (b) such entertainer or athlete is present in that other State for a period or periods aggregating more than 90 days in the fiscal year concerned.

2. Where income in respect of activities exercised by an entertainer or an athlete in his capacity as such accrues not to him but to another person, that income may, notwithstanding the provisions of Articles 7 (Business Profits), 14 (Independent Personal Services), and 15 (Dependent Personal Services), be taxed in the Contracting State in which the activities of the entertainer or athlete are exercised. For purposes of the preceding sentence, income of an entertainer or athlete shall be deemed not to accrue to another person if it is proved by the entertainer or athlete that neither he nor persons related to him participate directly or indirectly in the profits of such

other person in any manner, including the receipt of deferred remuneration, bonuses, fees, dividends, partnership distributions, or other distributions.

ARTICLE 18

Pensions, Etc.

1. Subject to the provisions of paragraph 2 of Article 19 (Government Service), pensions and other similar remuneration beneficially derived by a resident of a Contracting State in consideration of past employment shall be taxable only in that State.

2. Payments made by a Contracting State under provisions of the social security or similar legislation of that State to a resident of the other Contracting State shall be taxable only in the other State.

3. Notwithstanding the provisions of paragraph 1, if a resident of a Contracting State becomes a resident of the other Contracting State, lump-sum payments or severance payments (indemnities) received after such change of residence that are paid with respect to employment exercised in the first-mentioned State while a resident thereof, shall be taxable only in that first-mentioned State. For purposes of this paragraph, the term "severance payments (indemnities)" includes any payment made in consequence of the termination of any office or employment of a person.

4. Annuities beneficially derived by a resident of a Contracting State shall be taxable only in that State. The term "annuities" as used in this paragraph means a stated sum paid periodically at stated times during life or during a specified number of years, under an obligation to make the payments in return for adequate and full consideration in money or money's worth (other than services rendered).

5. Alimony and child support payments paid to a resident of a Contracting State by a resident of the other Contracting State shall be taxable only in the first-mentioned State. However, such payments shall not be taxable in either State if the person making such payments is not entitled to a deduction for such payments in the State of which he is a resident. The term

"alimony" as used in this paragraph means periodic payments made pursuant to a written separation agreement or a decree of divorce, separate maintenance, or compulsory support, which payments are taxable to the recipient under the laws of the State of which he is a resident. The term "child support" as used in this paragraph means periodic payments for the support of a minor child made pursuant to a written separation agreement or a decree of divorce, separate maintenance, or compulsory support.

6. For purposes of this Convention, where an individual who is a participant in a pension plan that is established and recognized under the legislation of one of the Contracting States performs personal services in the other Contracting State:

(a) Contributions paid by or on behalf of the individual to the plan during the period that he performs such services in the other State shall be deductible (or excludible) in computing his taxable income in that State. Any benefits accrued under the plan or payments made to the plan by or on behalf of his employer during that period shall not be treated as part of the employee's taxable income and shall be allowed as a deduction in computing the profits of his employer in that other State.

(b) The provisions of this paragraph shall apply only if:

(i) contributions by or on behalf of the individual to the plan (or to another similar plan for which this plan was substituted) were made before he arrived in the other State; and

(ii) the competent authority of the other State has agreed that the pension plan generally corresponds to a pension plan recognized for tax purposes by that State.

The benefits granted under this paragraph shall not exceed the benefits that would be allowed by the other State to its residents for contributions to, or benefits otherwise accrued under a pension plan recognized for tax purposes by that State.

ARTICLE 19

Government Service

1.   (a) Remuneration, other than a pension, paid by a Contracting State or a political or administrative subdivision or local authority thereof to an individual in respect of services rendered to that State or subdivision or authority shall be taxable only in that State.

(b) However, such remuneration shall be taxable only in the other Contracting State if the services are rendered in that State and the individual is a resident of that State who:

(i) is a national of that State and is not a national of the other State; or

(ii) did not become a resident of that State solely for the purpose of rendering the services;

provided that the provisions of clause (ii) shall not apply to the spouse or dependent children of an individual who is receiving remuneration to which the provisions of subparagraph (a) apply and who does not come within the terms of clause (i) or (ii).

2. Subject to the provisions of paragraph 2 of Article 18 (Pensions, Etc.):

(a) Any pension paid by, or out of funds created by, a Contracting State or a political or administrative subdivision or local authority thereof to an individual in respect of services rendered to that State or subdivision or local authority shall be taxable only in that State.

(b) However, such pension shall be taxable only in the other Contracting State if the individual is a resident and a national of that State.

3. The provisions of Article 14 (Independent Personal Services), 15 (Dependent Personal Services), 16 (Directors' Fees), 17 (Artistes and Athletes), or 18 (Pensions, Etc.), as the case may be, shall apply to remuneration and pensions in respect of services rendered in connection with a business

carried on by a Contracting State or a political or administrative subdivision or a local authority thereof.

ARTICLE 20

Professors and Teachers

1. A professor or teacher who makes a temporary visit to a Contracting State for a period that is not expected to exceed two years for the purpose of teaching or conducting research at a university, college, school, or other recognized educational institution, or at a medical facility primarily funded from governmental sources, and who is, or immediately before such visit was, a resident of the other Contracting State shall, for a period not exceeding two years, be exempt from tax in the first-mentioned Contracting State in respect of remuneration from such teaching or research.

2. This Article shall not apply to income from research if such research is undertaken not in the general interest but primarily for the private benefit of a specific person or persons.

ARTICLE 21

Students and Trainees

Payments which a student or business apprentice (trainee) who is, or immediately before visiting a Contracting State was, a resident of the other Contracting State and who is present in the first-mentioned State exclusively for the purpose of his education at a recognized educational institution or training receives for the purpose of his maintenance, education, or training shall not be taxed in that State provided that such payments arise outside that State.

ARTICLE 22

Other Income

1. Items of income of a resident of a Contracting State, wherever arising, not dealt with in the foregoing Articles of this Convention shall be taxable only in that State.

2. The provisions of paragraph 1 shall not apply to income, other than income from immovable property as defined in paragraph 2 of Article 6 (Income from Immovable Property), if the person deriving the income, being a resident of a Contracting State, carries on business in the other Contracting State through a permanent establishment situated therein, or performs in that other State independent personal services from a fixed base situated therein, and the right or property in respect of which the income if paid is effectively connected with such permanent establishment or fixed base. In such case the items of income are taxable in the other Contracting State according to its own law.

3. The provisions of this Article shall not apply if it was the main purpose or one of the main purposes of any person concerned with the creation or assignment of the rights in respect of which the income is paid to take advantage of this Article by means of that creation or assignment.

ARTICLE 23

Relief from Double Taxation

1. It is agreed that double taxation shall be avoided in accordance with the following paragraphs of this Article.

2.   (a) In accordance with the provisions and subject to the limitations of the law of the United States (as it may be amended from time to time without changing the general principle hereof), the United States shall allow to a resident or citizen of the United States as a credit against the United States tax on income the appropriate amount of income tax paid to Italy; and in the case of a United States company owning at least ten percent of the voting stock of a company which is a resident of Italy from which it receives dividends in any taxable year, the United

States shall allow as a credit against the United States tax on income the appropriate amount of income tax paid to Italy by that company with respect to the profits out of which such dividends are paid. Such appropriate amount shall be based upon the amount of tax paid to Italy, but shall not exceed the limitations of the law of the United States (for the purpose of limiting the credit to the United States tax on income from sources without the United States).

(b) For purposes of applying the United States credit in relation to tax paid to Italy, the taxes referred to in paragraphs 2(b)(i), 2(b)(ii) and 3 of Article 2 (Taxes Covered) shall be considered to be income taxes. In addition, for purposes of applying the United States credit in relation to tax paid to Italy, the portion of the tax referred to in paragraph 2(b)(iii) of Article 2 (Taxes Covered) as is described in subparagraph (c) of this paragraph shall be considered to be an income tax.

(c) The portion of the tax referred to in paragraph 2(b)(iii) of Article 2 (Taxes Covered) that shall be considered to be an income tax shall be calculated by multiplying the applicable ratio by the total amount of the tax referred to in paragraph 2(b)(iii) of Article 2 (Taxes Covered) that is paid or accrued to Italy.

(i) The term "applicable ratio" means the adjusted base divided by the total tax base upon which the tax referred to in paragraph 2(b)(iii) of Article 2 (Taxes Covered) is actually imposed.

(ii) The term "adjusted base" means the greater of:

(A) zero (0), or

(B) the total tax base upon which the tax referred to in paragraph 2(b)(iii) of Article 2 (Taxes Covered) is actually imposed, less the total amount of labor expense and interest expense not otherwise taken into account in determining the total tax base upon which the tax referred to in paragraph 2(b)(iii) of Article 2 (Taxes Covered) is actually imposed.

3. If a resident of Italy derives items of income which are taxable in the United States under the Convention (without regard to paragraph 2(b) of Article 1 (Personal Scope)), Italy may, in determining its income taxes specified in Article 2 of this Convention, include in the basis upon which such taxes are imposed the said items of income (unless specified provisions of this Convention otherwise provide). In such case, Italy shall deduct from the taxes so calculated the tax on income paid to the United States, but in an amount not exceeding that proportion of the aforesaid Italian tax which such items of income bear to the entire income. However, no deduction will be granted if the item of income is subjected in Italy to a final withholding tax by request of the recipient of the said income in accordance with Italian law. For purposes of applying the Italian credit in relation to tax paid to the United States the taxes referred to in paragraphs 2(a) and 3 of Article 2 (Taxes Covered) shall be considered to be income taxes.

4. Where a United States citizen is a resident of Italy:

(a) with respect to items of income that under the provisions of this Convention are exempt from United States tax or that are subject to a reduced rate of United States tax when derived by a resident of Italy who is not a United States citizen, Italy shall allow as a credit against Italian tax an amount not exceeding the tax that would be due to the United States if the resident of Italy were not a citizen of the United States;

(b) for purposes of computing United States tax on those items of income referred to in subparagraph (a), the United States shall allow as a credit against United States tax the income tax paid to Italy after the credit referred to in subparagraph (a); the credit so allowed shall not reduce the portion of the United States tax that is creditable against the Italian tax in accordance with subparagraph (a); and

(c) for the exclusive purpose of relieving double taxation in the United States under subparagraph (b), items of income referred to in subparagraph (a) shall be deemed to arise in Italy to the extent necessary to avoid double taxation of such income under subparagraph (b).

5. In the case of an individual who is both a resident and national of one Contracting State and is also a national of the other Contracting State, the provisions of paragraph 2 of Article 1 (Personal Scope) shall apply to remuneration described in paragraph 1(b)(i) of Article 19 (Government Service), but such remuneration shall be treated by the Contracting State where the services in respect of the remuneration are rendered as income from sources within the other State.

ARTICLE 24

Non-Discrimination

1. Nationals of a Contracting State shall not be subjected in the other State to any taxation or any requirement connected therewith, which is other or more burdensome than the taxation and connected requirements to which nationals of that other State in the same circumstances are or may be subjected. This provision shall, notwithstanding the provisions of Article 1 (Personal Scope), also apply to persons who are not residents of one or both of the Contracting States. However, for purposes of United States taxation, United States citizens who are subject to tax on a worldwide basis are not in the same circumstances as Italian nationals who are not residents of the United States.

2. The taxation on a permanent establishment which an enterprise of a Contracting State has in the other Contracting State shall not be less favorably levied in that other State than the taxation levied on enterprises of that other State carrying on the same activities. This provision shall not be construed as obliging a Contracting State to grant to residents of the other State any personal allowances, reliefs, and reductions for taxation purposes on account of civil status or family responsibilities which it grants to its own residents.

3. Except where the provisions of paragraph 1 of Article 9 (Associated Enterprises), paragraph 7 of Article 11 (Interest), or paragraph 7 of Article 12 (Royalties) apply, interest, royalties, and all other disbursements paid by an enterprise of a Contracting State to a resident of the other Contracting State shall, for the purpose of determining the taxable profits of such enterprise, be deductible under the same conditions as if they had been paid to a resident of the first-mentioned State.

4. Enterprises of a Contracting State, the capital of which is wholly or partly owned or controlled, directly or indirectly, by one or more residents of the other Contracting State shall not be subjected in the first-mentioned State to any taxation or any requirement connected therewith which is other or more burdensome than the taxation and connected requirements to which other similar enterprises of the first-mentioned State are or may be subjected.

5. For purposes of this Article, notwithstanding the provisions of Article 2 (Taxes Covered), this Convention shall apply to taxes of every kind and description imposed by a Contracting State or a political or administrative subdivision or local authority thereof.

ARTICLE 25

Mutual Agreement Procedure

1. Where a person considers that the actions of one or both of the Contracting States result or will result for him in taxation not in accordance with the provisions of this Convention, he may, irrespective of the remedies provided by the domestic law of those States, present his case to the competent authority of the Contracting State of which he is a resident or, if his case comes under paragraph 1 of Article 24 (Non-Discrimination), to that of the Contracting State of which he is a national. The case must be presented within three years from the first notification of the action resulting in taxation not in accordance with the provisions of the Convention.

2. The competent authority shall endeavor, if the objection appears to it to be justified and if it is not itself able to arrive at a satisfactory solution, to resolve the case by mutual agreement with the competent authority of the other Contracting State, with a view to the avoidance of taxation which is not in accordance with the Convention. Any agreement reached shall be implemented notwithstanding any time limits in the domestic law of the Contracting States.

3. The competent authorities of the Contracting States shall endeavor to resolve by mutual agreement any difficulties or doubts arising as to the interpretation or application of the

Convention. They may also consult together for the elimination of double taxation in cases not provided for in the Convention.

4. The competent authorities of the Contracting States may communicate with each other directly for the purpose of reaching an agreement in the sense of the preceding paragraphs. When it seems advisable in order to reach agreement to have an oral exchange of opinions, such exchange may take place through a Commission consisting of representatives of the competent authorities of the Contracting States.

5. If an agreement cannot be reached by the competent authorities pursuant to the previous paragraphs of this Article, the case may, if both competent authorities and the taxpayer agree, be submitted for arbitration, provided that the taxpayer agrees in writing to be bound by the decision of the arbitration board. The competent authorities may release to the arbitration board such information as is necessary for carrying out the arbitration procedure. The award of the arbitration board shall be binding on the taxpayer and on both States with regard to that case. The procedures shall be finalized by the Contracting States by means of notes to be exchanged through diplomatic channels after consultation between the competent authorities. The provisions of this paragraph shall not have effect until the date specified in the exchange of diplomatic notes.

ARTICLE 26

Exchange of Information

1. The competent authorities of the Contracting States shall exchange such information as is necessary for carrying out the provisions of this Convention or of the domestic laws of the Contracting States concerning taxes covered by the Convention insofar as the taxation thereunder is not contrary to the Convention, and for the prevention of fraud or fiscal evasion. The exchange of information is not restricted by Article 1 (Personal Scope). Any information received by a Contracting State shall be treated as secret in the same manner as information obtained under the domestic laws of that State and shall be disclosed only to persons or authorities (including courts and administrative bodies) involved in the assessment or collection of, the enforcement or prosecution in respect of, or the determination of appeals in relation to, the taxes covered

by the Convention. Such persons or authorities shall use the information only for such purposes. They may disclose the information in public court proceedings or in judicial decisions.

2. In no case shall the provisions of paragraph 1 be construed so as to impose on a Contracting State the obligation:

(a) to carry out administrative measures at variance with the laws and administrative practice of that or of the other Contracting State;

(b) to supply information which is not obtainable under the laws or in the normal course of the administration of that or of the other Contracting State;

(c) to supply information which would disclose any trade, business, industrial, commercial, or professional secret or trade process, or information, the disclosure of which would be contrary to public policy (ordre public).

ARTICLE 27

Diplomatic Agents and Consular Officials

Nothing in this Convention shall affect the fiscal privileges of diplomatic agents or consular officials under the general rules of international law or under the provisions of special agreements.

ARTICLE 28

Entry into Force

1. This Convention shall be subject to ratification in accordance with the applicable procedures of each Contracting State and instruments of ratification shall be exchanged as soon as possible.

2. The Convention shall enter into force upon the exchange of instruments of ratification and its provisions shall have effect:

(a) in respect of tax withheld at the source, for amounts paid or credited on or after the first day of the second month following the date on which this Convention enters into force,

(b) in respect of other taxes, for taxable periods beginning on or after the first day of January next following the date on which this Convention enters into force.

3. Notwithstanding paragraph 2, where a person who was entitled to the benefits of the Convention for the Avoidance of Double Taxation with Respect to Taxes on Income and the Prevention of Fraud or Fiscal Evasion, signed at Rome April 17, 1984, and the Protocol clarifying and supplementing that Convention, signed at Rome April 17, 1984 (collectively, the "prior Convention") would have been entitled to any greater relief from tax under the prior Convention than under this Convention, the prior Convention shall, at the election of such person, continue to have effect in its entirety for a twelve-month period from the date on which the provisions of this Convention would otherwise have effect under paragraph 2.

4. The provisions of the prior Convention shall cease to have effect when corresponding provisions of this Convention take effect in accordance with paragraphs 2 and 3, and the prior Convention shall terminate on the last date on which it has effect in accordance with the foregoing provisions of this paragraph.

ARTICLE 29

Termination

This Convention shall remain in force until terminated by one of the Contracting States. Either Contracting State may terminate the Convention at any time after 5 years from the date on which this Convention enters into force provided that at least 6 months' prior notice of termination has been given through diplomatic channels. In such event, the Convention shall cease to have effect:

(a) in respect of tax withheld at the source, for amounts paid or credited on or after the first day of

January next following the expiration of the 6 months'
period;

     (b) in respect of other taxes, for taxable periods
beginning on or after the first day of January next
following the expiration of the 6 months' period.

     IN WITNESS WHEREOF, the undersigned, being duly authorized
by their respective Governments, have signed this Convention.

     DONE at Washington, in duplicate, in the English and
Italian languages, the two texts having equal authenticity, this
twenty-fifth day of August, 1999.

FOR THE GOVERNMENT OF THE   FOR THE GOVERNMENT OF THE
UNITED STATES OF AMERICA: ITALIAN REPUBLIC:

PROTOCOL

The Government of the United States of America and the Government of the Italian Republic, desiring to conclude a Protocol clarifying and supplementing the Convention for the Avoidance of Double Taxation with Respect to Taxes on Income and the Prevention of Fraud or Fiscal Evasion (hereinafter referred to as "the Convention") to be signed simultaneously with the signing of this Protocol, have agreed upon the following provisions, which shall be an integral part of the Convention.

ARTICLE 1

1. For purposes of paragraph 2(b) of Article 1 (Personal Scope) of the Convention, the term "citizen" as applied to the United States shall include a former citizen or long-term resident whose loss of such status had as one of its principal purposes the avoidance of tax, but only for a period of 10 years following such loss.

2. The provisions of paragraph 2 of Article 1 (Personal Scope) of the Convention shall not affect:

(a) the benefits conferred by a Contracting State under paragraph 2 of Article 18 (Pensions, Etc.) of the Convention to residents of the other Contracting State who are nationals of that other State, even if they are also nationals of the first-mentioned State;

(b) the benefits conferred by a Contracting State under Article 4 of this Protocol.

3. For purposes of paragraph 2(a) of Article 2 (Taxes Covered) of the Convention, the Convention shall apply to the excise tax imposed by the United States on insurance premiums paid to foreign insurers only to the extent that the foreign insurer does not reinsure such risks with a person not entitled to exemption from such tax under this or any other Convention.

4. For purposes of paragraph 1(i) of Article 3 (General Definitions) of the Convention, the term "qualified governmental entity" includes:

    (a) in the case of the United States:

        (i) the Federal Reserve Banks;

        (ii) the Export-Import Bank; and

        (iii) the Overseas Private Investment Corporation;

    (b) in the case of Italy:

        (i) La Banca d'Italia (the Central Bank);

        (ii) L'Istituto per il Commercio con l'Estero (the Foreign Trade Institute); and

        (iii) L'Istituto per l'Assicurazione del Credito all'Esportazione (the Official Insurance Institute for Export Credits);

and such financial institutions, the capital of which is wholly owned by a Contracting State or any state or political or administrative subdivision or local authority as may be agreed from time to time between the competent authorities of both of the Contracting States.

5. For purposes of paragraph 1 of Article 4 (Resident) of the Convention:

    (a) A legal person organized under the laws of a Contracting State and that is generally exempt from tax in that State and is established and maintained in that State either:

        (i) exclusively for a religious, charitable, educational, scientific, or other similar purpose; or

        (ii) to provide pensions or other similar benefits to employees pursuant to a plan

is to be treated as a resident of that Contracting State;

(b) A qualified governmental entity is to be treated as a resident of the Contracting State where it is established;

(c) Italy shall treat a United States citizen or an alien lawfully admitted for permanent residence (a "green card" holder) as a resident of the United States only if such person has a substantial presence, permanent home, or habitual abode in the United States; and

(d) The provisions of subparagraph 1(b) of Article 4 (Resident) of the Convention shall apply to determine the residence of an entity that is treated as fiscally transparent under the laws of either Contracting State.

6. For purposes of paragraph 2 of Article 5 (Permanent Establishment) of the Convention, a drilling rig or ship used for the exploration or development of natural resources constitutes a permanent establishment in a Contracting State only if it remains in that State for more than twelve months.

7. For purposes of paragraph 1 of Article 8 (Shipping and Air Transport) of the Convention, profits from the operation in international traffic of ships or aircraft include:

(a) profits from the use, maintenance, or rental of containers (including trailers, barges, and related equipment for the transport of containers) used for the transport in international traffic of goods or merchandise; and

(b) profits derived from the rental on a full basis of ships or aircraft and profits derived from the rental on a bareboat basis of ships or aircraft, provided in the latter case that such rental profits are incidental to other profits from the operation of ships or aircraft in international traffic.

8. For purposes of Article 8 (Shipping and Air Transport) of the Convention, and notwithstanding any other provision of the Convention, profits which a national of the United States not resident in Italy or a United States corporation derives from operating ships documented or aircraft registered under the laws of the United States shall be exempt from tax in Italy.

9. The provisions of Article 9 (Associated Enterprises) of the Convention shall not limit any provisions of the law of either Contracting State which permit the distribution, apportionment, or allocation of income, deductions, credits, or allowances between persons owned or controlled directly or indirectly by the same interests when necessary in order to prevent evasion of taxes or clearly to reflect the income of any such persons.

10. For purposes of paragraph 4 of Article 10 (Dividends), paragraph 5 of Article 11 (Interest), paragraph 5 of Article 12 (Royalties), and paragraph 2 of Article 22 (Other Income) of the Convention, it is agreed that the last sentence included therein cannot be interpreted so that the principles included in Articles 7 (Business Profits) and 14 (Independent Personal Services) of the Convention are not taken into consideration.

11. Notwithstanding the provisions of paragraphs 1, 2, and 3 of Article 11 (Interest) of the Convention, interest that is an excess inclusion with respect to a real estate mortgage investment conduit may be taxed by each State in accordance with its own domestic law.

12. For purposes of paragraph 1 of Article 13 (Capital Gains) of the Convention:

    (a) the term "immovable property" in the case of the United States, includes a United States real property interest; and

    (b) the term "immovable property" in the case of Italy includes:

        (i) immovable property referred to in Article 6 (Income from Immovable Property);

        (ii) shares or comparable interests in a company or other body of persons, the assets of which consist wholly or principally of real property situated in Italy; and

        (iii) an interest in an estate of a deceased individual, the assets of which consist wholly or principally of real property situated in Italy.

(c) property described in subparagraph (a) of this paragraph shall be deemed to be situated in the United States and property described in subparagraph (b) of this paragraph shall be deemed to be situated in Italy.

13. For purposes of paragraph 3 of Article 13 (Capital Gains) of the Convention, gains derived by an enterprise of a Contracting State from the alienation of ships or aircraft operated by such enterprise in international traffic include:

(a) gains from the alienation of containers (including trailers, barges, and related equipment for the transport of containers) used for the transport in international traffic of goods or merchandise; and

(b) gains from the alienation of ships or aircraft rented on a full basis or gains from the alienation of ships or aircraft rented on a bareboat basis if, in the latter case, rental profits were incidental to other profits from the operation of ships or aircraft in international traffic.

14. Directors' fees and other similar payments derived by a resident of a Contracting State which are described in Article 16 (Directors' Fees) of the Convention may be taxed in the other Contracting State only to the extent that the fees and other payments are attributable to services performed in such other State.

15. With respect to paragraph 6 of Article 18 (Pensions, Etc.), the term "pension plan" in the case of Italy shall mean "fondi pensione."

16. With respect to Article 19 (Government Service) of the Convention, it is understood that the competent authorities of the Contracting States may by mutual agreement apply the provisions of paragraphs 1 and 2 of Article 19 (Government Service) to employees of organizations that perform functions of a governmental nature.

17. With respect to Articles 20 (Professors and Teachers) and 21 (Students and Trainees) of the Convention, the term "recognized educational institution" in the case of the United States shall mean an accredited educational institution. An educational institution will be considered to be accredited if it is accredited by an authority that generally is responsible

for accreditation of institutions in the particular field of study.

18. Nothing in Article 24 (Non-Discrimination) of the Convention shall be construed as preventing either Contracting State from imposing a tax as described in paragraph 6 of Article 10 (Dividends) or paragraph 8 of Article 11 (Interest) of the Convention.

19. With respect to paragraph 3 of Article 25 (Mutual Agreement Procedure) of the Convention, the competent authorities of the Contracting States may, in particular, agree that the conditions for the application of paragraph 10 of Article 10 (Dividends), paragraph 9 of Article 11 (Interest), paragraph 8 of Article 12 (Royalties), or paragraph 3 of Article 22 (Other Income) of the Convention are met.

20. For purposes of Article 26 (Exchange of Information) of the Convention, the Convention shall apply to taxes of every kind imposed by a Contracting State. It is understood that information may be disclosed to persons or authorities involved in the oversight of the activities for which information may be exchanged under Article 26 (Exchange of Information), and such persons shall use the information only for such oversight purposes and shall be subject to the limitations of Article 26 (Exchange of Information).

ARTICLE 2

1. A resident of a Contracting State shall be entitled to benefits otherwise accorded to residents of a Contracting State by the Convention only to the extent provided in this Article.

2. A resident of a Contracting State shall be entitled to all the benefits of the Convention if the resident is:

   (a) an individual;

   (b) a qualified governmental entity;

   (c) a company, if:

      (i) all the shares in the class or classes of shares representing more than 50 percent of the voting power and value of the company are regularly traded on a recognized stock exchange, or

(ii) at least 50 percent of each class of shares in the company is owned directly or indirectly by five or fewer companies entitled to benefits under clause (i), provided that in the case of indirect ownership, each intermediate owner is a person entitled to benefits of the Convention under this paragraph;

(d) described in subparagraph 5(a)(i) of Article 1 of this Protocol;

(e) described in subparagraph 5(a)(ii) of Article 1 of this Protocol, provided that more than 50 percent of the person's beneficiaries, members or participants are individuals resident in either Contracting State; or

(f) a person other than an individual, if:

(i) On at least half the days of the taxable year persons described in subparagraphs (a), (b), (c), (d) or (e) own, directly or indirectly (through a chain of ownership in which each person is entitled to benefits of the Convention under this paragraph), at least 50 percent of each class of shares or other beneficial interests in the person, and

(ii) less than 50 percent of the person's gross income for the taxable year is paid or accrued, directly or indirectly, to persons who are not residents of either Contracting State (unless the payment is attributable to a permanent establishment situated in either State), in the form of payments that are deductible for income tax purposes in the person's State of residence.

3. (a) A resident of a Contracting State not otherwise entitled to benefits shall be entitled to the benefits of this Convention with respect to an item of income derived from the other State, if:

(i) the resident is engaged in the active conduct of a trade or business in the first-mentioned State,

(ii) the income is connected with or incidental to the trade or business, and

(iii) the trade or business is substantial in relation to the activity in the other State generating the income.

(b) For purposes of this paragraph, the business of making or managing investments will not be considered an active trade or business unless the activity is banking, insurance or securities activity conducted by a bank, insurance company or registered securities dealer.

(c) Whether a trade or business is substantial for purposes of this paragraph will be determined based on all the facts and circumstances. In any case, however, a trade or business will be deemed substantial if, for the preceding taxable year, or for the average of the three preceding taxable years, the asset value, the gross income, and the payroll expense that are related to the trade or business in the first-mentioned State equal at least 7.5 percent of the resident's (and any related parties') proportionate share of the asset value, gross income and payroll expense, respectively, that are related to the activity that generated the income in the other State, and the average of the three ratios exceeds 10 percent.

(d) Income is derived in connection with a trade or business if the activity in the other State generating the income is a line of business that forms a part of or is complementary to the trade or business. Income is incidental to a trade or business if it facilitates the conduct of the trade or business in the other State.

4. A resident of a Contracting State not otherwise entitled to benefits may be granted benefits of the Convention if the competent authority of the State from which benefits are claimed so determines.

5. For purposes of this Article the term "recognized stock exchange" means:

(a) the NASDAQ System owned by the National Association of Securities Dealers, Inc. and any stock exchange registered with the U.S. Securities and Exchange Commission as a national securities exchange under the U.S. Securities Exchange Act of 1934;

(b) any stock exchange constituted and organized according to Italian laws; and

(c) any other stock exchanges agreed upon by the competent authorities of both Contracting States.

ARTICLE 3

1. The Convention shall not restrict in any manner any exclusion, exemption, deduction, credit, or other allowance now or hereafter accorded:

(a) by the laws of either Contracting State, or

(b) by any other agreement between the Contracting States.

2. Notwithstanding the provisions of paragraph 1(b):

(a) the provisions of Article 25 (Mutual Agreement Procedure) of the Convention exclusively shall apply to any dispute concerning whether a measure is within the scope of the Convention, and the procedures under the Convention exclusively shall apply to that dispute; and

(b) unless the competent authorities determine that a taxation measure is not within the scope of this Convention, the nondiscrimination obligations of this Convention exclusively shall apply with respect to that measure, except for such national treatment or most-favored-nation obligations as may apply to trade in goods under the General Agreement on Tariffs and Trade. No national treatment or most-favored-nation obligation under any other agreement shall apply with respect to that measure.

(c) For the purpose of this paragraph, a "measure" is a law, regulation, rule, procedure, decision, administrative action, or any similar provision or action.

ARTICLE 4

It is agreed that a United States citizen resident in Italy who is a partner of a partnership that is a national of the United States shall be entitled to a refundable credit against that partner's individual income tax (l'imposta sul reddito delle persone fisiche) imposed by Italy for the taxable period equal to the portion of the corporation income tax (l'imposta sul reddito delle persone giuridiche) imposed by Italy for the same period on the partnership that is attributable to that partner's share of the partnership income.

ARTICLE 5

Taxes withheld at the source in a Contracting State at the rates provided by domestic law will be refunded by request of the taxpayer if the right to collect the said taxes is limited by the provisions of the Convention. Claims for refund, which shall be made within the time limit fixed by the law of the Contracting State which is obliged to make the refund, shall be accompanied by an official certificate of the Contracting State of which the taxpayer is a resident certifying the existence of the conditions required for being entitled to the benefits provided for by the Convention. This provision shall not be construed to prevent the competent authority of each Contracting State from establishing other modes of application of the benefits provided for by the Convention.

ARTICLE 6

Each of the Contracting States may collect on behalf of the other Contracting State such amounts as may be necessary to ensure that relief granted by the Convention from taxation imposed by such other State does not enure to the benefit of persons not entitled thereto. The preceding sentence shall not, however, impose upon either of the Contracting States the obligation to carry out administrative measures which are of a different nature from those used in the collection of its own tax, or which would be contrary to its sovereignty, security, or public policy.

ARTICLE 7

1.   The appropriate authority of either Contracting State may request consultations with the appropriate authority of the other Contracting State to determine whether amendment to the Convention is appropriate to respond to changes in the law or policy of either Contracting State. If these consultations determine that the effect of the Convention or its application have been unilaterally changed by reason of domestic legislation enacted by a Contracting State such that the balance of benefits provided by the Convention has been significantly altered, the authorities shall consult with each other with a view to amending the Convention to restore an appropriate balance of benefits.

2. Within three years after the entry into force of the Convention, the competent authorities shall consult with respect to the implementation of Article 25 (Mutual Agreement Procedure) and, taking into account experience with respect thereto, determine whether any modifications to Article 25 (Mutual Agreement Procedure) would be appropriate and, also taking into account experience with respect to arbitration of international tax disputes, shall determine whether it is appropriate to exchange the diplomatic notes referred to in paragraph 5 of Article 25 (Mutual Agreement Procedure), and if so the provisions thereof.

ARTICLE 8

If any State or locality of the United States imposes tax on profits of enterprises of Italy from the operation in international traffic of ships or aircraft, Italy may impose its regional tax on productive activities (l'imposta regionale sulle attività produttive) on such profits of enterprises of the United States, notwithstanding the provisions of subparagraph 2(b)(iii) of Article 2 (Taxes Covered) and Article 8 (Shipping and Air Transport) of the Convention.

IN WITNESS WHEREOF, the undersigned, being duly authorized by their respective Governments, have signed this Protocol.

DONE at Washington, in duplicate, in the English and Italian languages, the two texts having equal authenticity, this twenty-fifth day of August, 1999.

FOR THE GOVERNMENT OF THE
UNITED STATES OF AMERICA:

FOR THE GOVERNMENT OF THE
ITALIAN REPUBLIC: